Richard Scarry's

Best Word Book Ever

D1080708

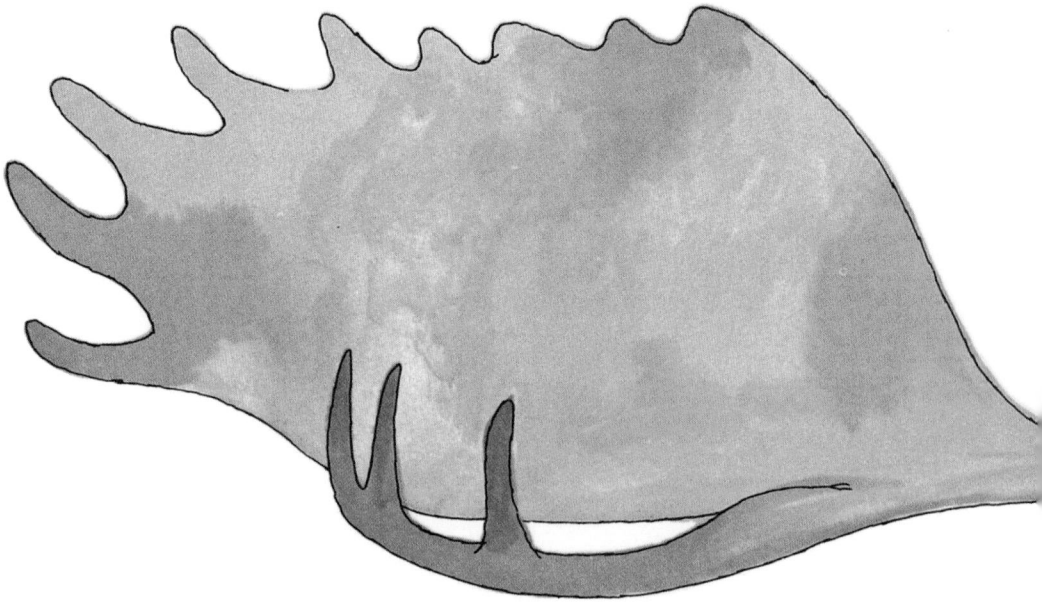

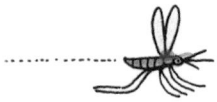

mosquito

First published in hardback in the UK by HarperCollins *Publishers* in 1980
This edition published by HarperCollins *Children's Books* in 2013

HarperCollins *Children's Books* is a division of HarperCollins *Publishers* Ltd,
77-85 Fulham Palace Road, London W6 8JB

1 3 5 7 9 10 8 6 4 2

ISBN: 978-0-00-750709-2

© 1963 renewed 1991 Golden Books Publishing Company, Inc.
New illustrations © 1980 Richard Scarry.
All rights reserved
No part of this publication may be reproduced, stored in a retrieval system or transmitted in any form or by any means, electronic, mechanical, photocopying, recording or otherwise, without the prior permission of HarperCollins *Publishers* Ltd, 77-85 Fulham Palace Road, London W6 8JB.

The HarperCollins website address is www.harpercollins.co.uk

Printed and bound in China.

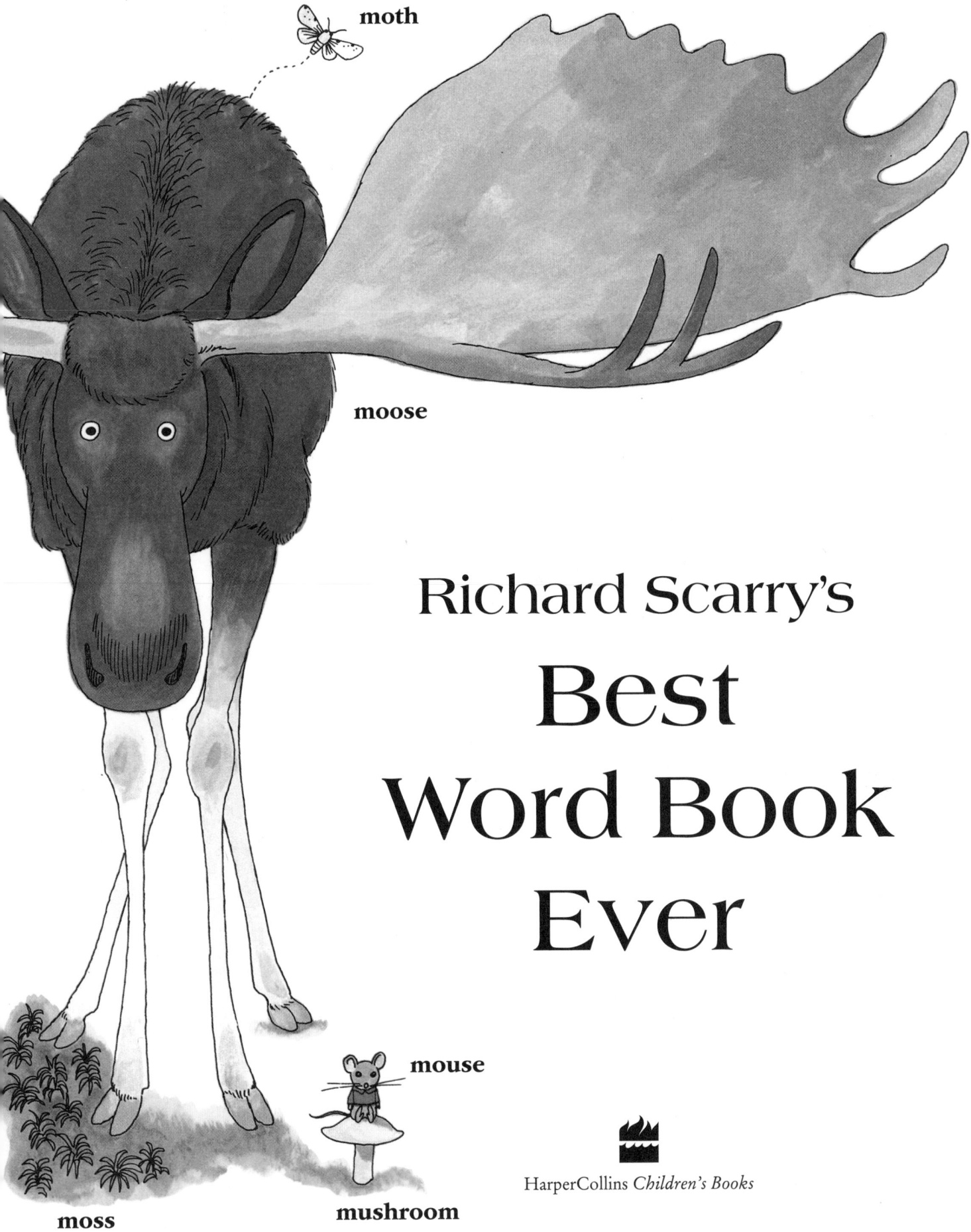

Richard Scarry's Best Word Book Ever

HarperCollins *Children's Books*

The Alphabet

The alligator is eating an apple.
The goose is wearing gloves.
What is the xiphias doing?

A alligator

B bear

C cat

D dog

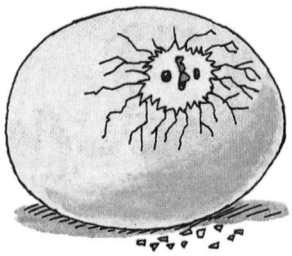

E egg

F fish

G goose

H heart

I ice cream cone

J jacket

K kangaroo

L letter

M mailbag

N nut

O owl

P present

Q queen

R rug

S spider

T turtle

U umbrella

V vase

W walrus

X xiphias

xylophone

Y yarn

Z zip

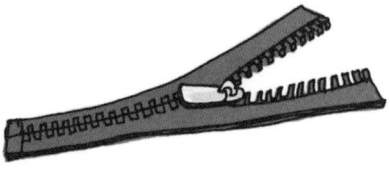

The New Day

It is the morning of a new day.
The sun is shining.
Kenny Bear gets up out of bed.

First he washes his face and hands.

Then he brushes his teeth.

He combs his hair.

He dresses himself.

He makes his bed.

He goes to the kitchen to eat his breakfast.

Kenny Bear sits in
his favourite chair.

He is very hungry.
This is what he eats —

cold fruit juice

warm cereal

with milk

pancakes

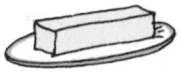

with butter and maple syrup

He doesn't
eat the
toaster.

fried eggs

bacon

toast

muffins

honey

jam

hot chocolate

cool milk

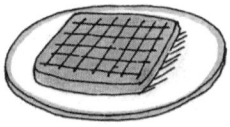

and a waffle.

When he finishes eating breakfast he
helps wash and dry the dishes.

cup

saucer

plate

bowl

fork

knife

spoon

tumbler

jar

jug

frying pan

lid

saucepan

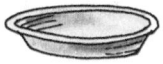

pan

bottle

juice squeezer

glass

Now he is ready to play with his friends.

The Rabbit Family's House

Father Rabbit, Mother Rabbit and the Rabbit children are getting ready for the new day. Their friend Owl is waiting for the children to come outside. Can you find him?

smoke
WHOO
owl
aerial
light switch
television
foot stool
record player
Mickey
bunk bed
bathroom
landing
Molly
bedroom
front door
living room
outside light
candle
picture
telephone
fireplace
stairs
sofa or couch
hall
doormat
rug
window
stone path

Painting and Drawing with Colours

Painting and drawing are fun. You can use bright colours. You can paint with brushes or even your fingers. You can draw with crayons or pencils. What do you like to draw?

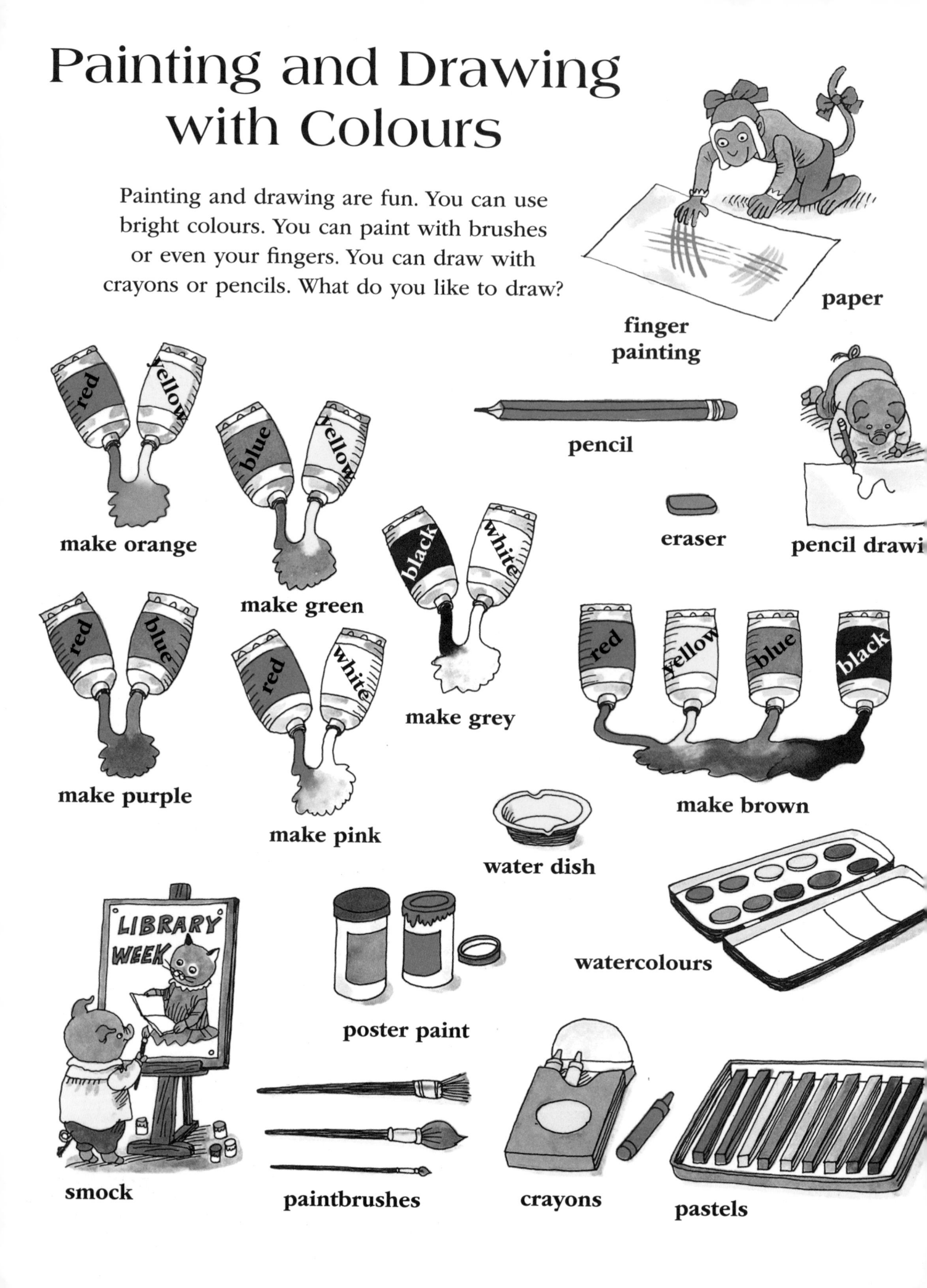

Toys

Sometimes it is fun to play by yourself. Sometimes it is fun to play with your friends. What are your favourite toys? Do you like to play with blocks?

tricycle

rocking horse

electric train set

truck and loader

blocks

scooter

glider

robot

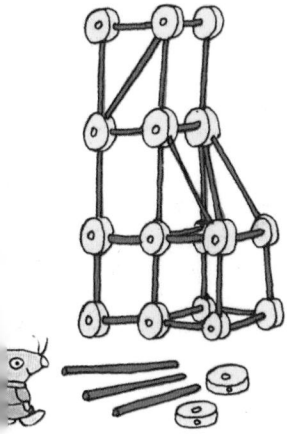

building set

croquet

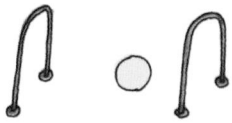

At the Playground

The children are all having fun doing different things. Which children are doing the things you like best?

climbing frame
kite
bubble blowing
merry-go-round
LISA
tag
ring toss
hoop rolling
jacks
marbles
sandpit
kite string
bouncing ball
hopscotch
1
2
3
4
5
6
7
8

hammer
Tools
nail
Everyone is very busy working with tools. What tools do you have in your house? What would you like to build?
pushpin
axe
ladder
log
carpenter
board
saw
sandpaper
sawdust
hacksaw
drill
vice
plane
woodpecker
wood shavings
jigsaw
screwdriver
screws
file
pliers

bucksaw
bricklayer
trowel
hoe
brick
brick wall
cement
timber
paintbrush
fence painter
ball of string
sawhorse
paint
ruler
barrel
tack
tack hammer
axe
folding ruler
penknife
toolbox
square
putty knife
shovel
bolt
nut
dirt
monkey wrench
mpass
wheelbarrow
pick
glue

crow
scarecrow
weather vane
N
W
E
S
silo
field
tractor
hayloft
barn
goat
stall
tin can
milk can
bucket
farm lorry
wagon
hen
cockerel
pigsty
baby chick
Kathy Bear is going to feed the pig.

The Bears' Farm

The Bears are working hard on their farm. What are they all doing? What is the duck doing? What is the scarecrow supposed to be doing? He is not doing it, is he?

At the Airport

The air traffic controller is talking to the pilot of the jet passenger plane. The controller is giving the pilot take-off instructions.

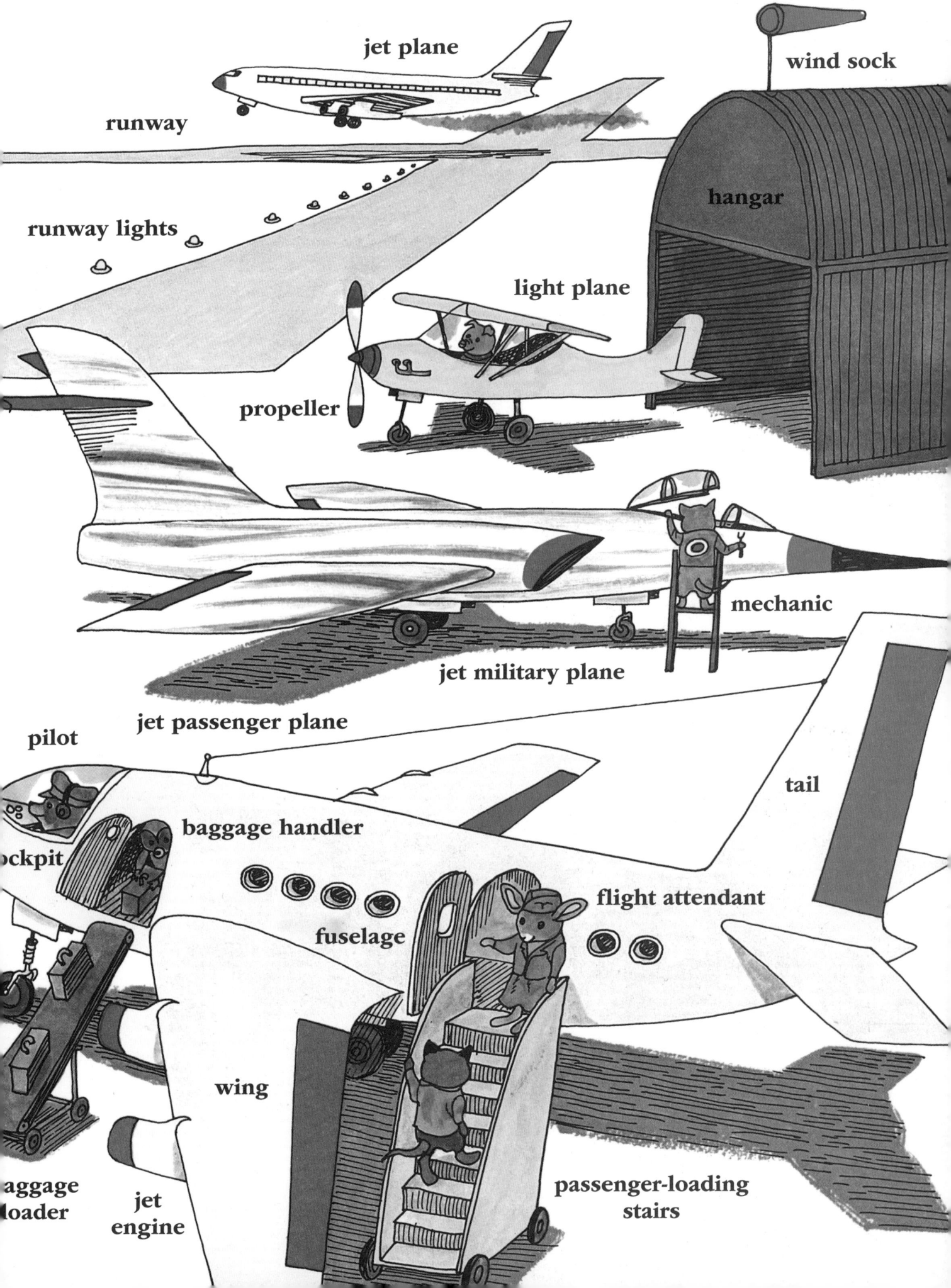
jet plane
wind sock
runway
hangar
runway lights
light plane
propeller
mechanic
jet military plane
jet passenger plane
pilot
tail
baggage handler
ockpit
flight attendant
fuselage
wing
aggage
loader
jet
engine
passenger-loading
stairs

At the Supermarket

The Pigs are buying groceries for their family.
What would you like to buy the next time
you go to the supermarket?
Would you like to buy a pickle?

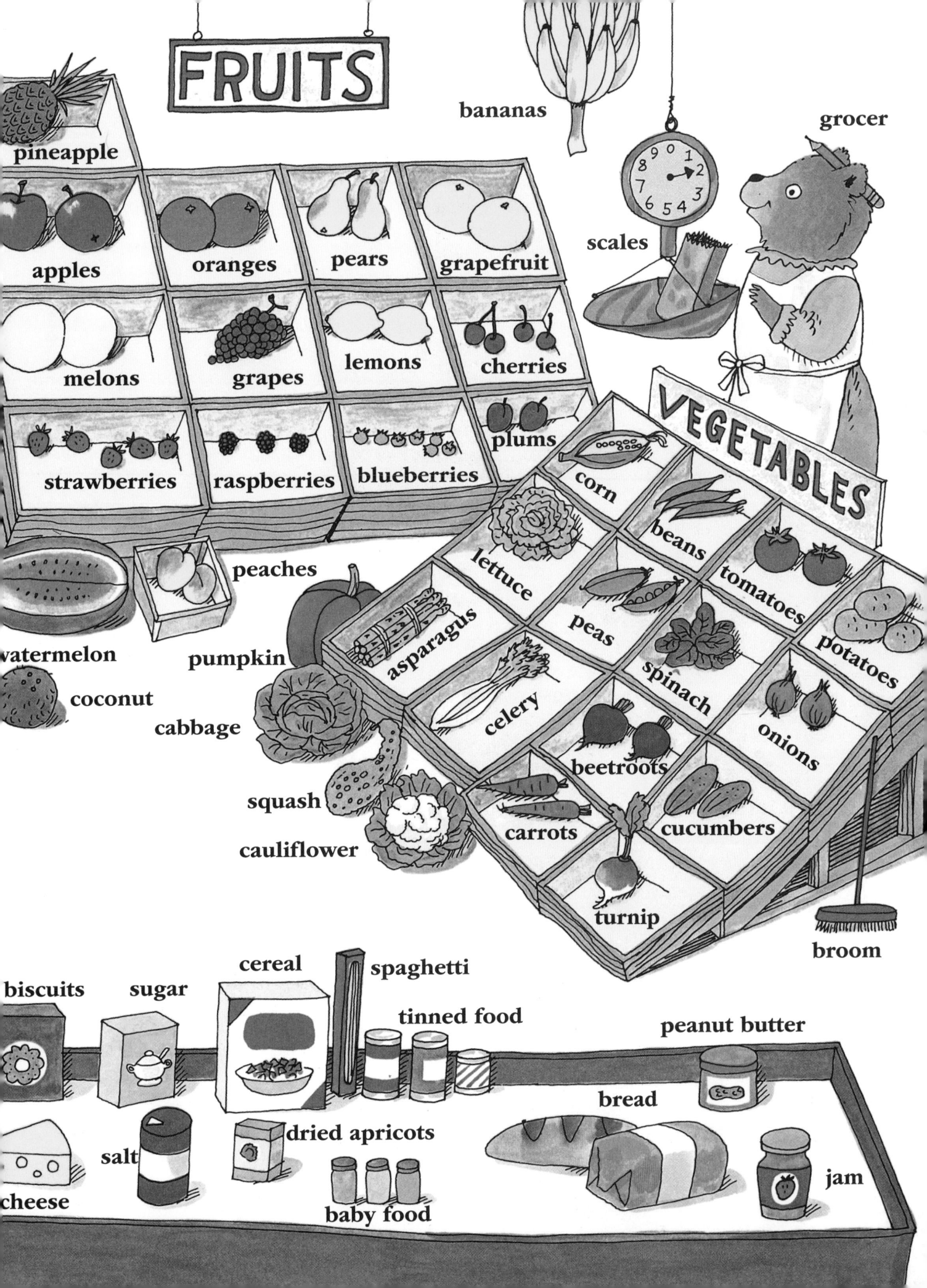
FRUITS
bananas
grocer
pineapple
scales
apples
oranges
pears
grapefruit
melons
grapes
lemons
cherries
strawberries
raspberries
blueberries
plums
VEGETABLES
corn
beans
lettuce
tomatoes
peaches
peas
asparagus
potatoes
watermelon
pumpkin
spinach
coconut
celery
onions
cabbage
beetroots
squash
carrots
cucumbers
cauliflower
turnip
broom
biscuits
sugar
cereal
spaghetti
tinned food
peanut butter
bread
salt
dried apricots
jam
cheese
baby food

Meal time

The Pig family is having
a special celebration meal.
There is so much good
food to enjoy!
What do you see on the
table that you like to eat?

turkey
milk jug
cake
pumpkin mash
baked potatoes
green beans
jelly
cranberry sauce
mashed potatoes
onions
beetroots
ice cream
steak
peas
butter
soup
pie
salad
white bread
brown bread
rolls

Boats and Ships

One of the things in the water is not a boat, but it helps boats to find the place they want to go. Do you know what it is?

freighter
lightship
AMBROSE
CG-7
coast guard ship
l tanker
F.D.
fireboat
ishing nets
fishing trawler
sport-fishing boat
10
speedboat
houseboat
raft
THE WHITE SWAN
sailing boat
2
light buoy

Keeping Healthy

Your doctor and your dentist are your good friends.
They want you to stay healthy and strong.
Will you give your doctor and dentist a big smile the next time you see them? How big a smile can you smile?

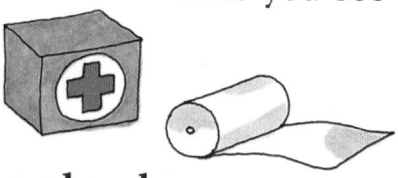

gauze bandage

adhesive tape

thermometer

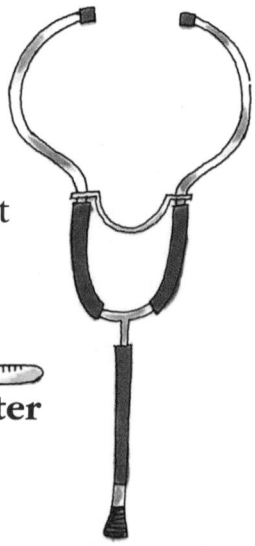

stethoscope

cotton wool

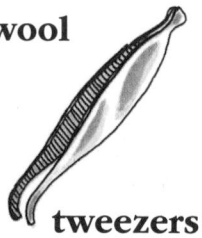

tweezers

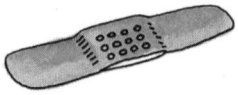

plaster for small cuts and hurts

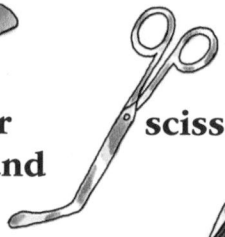

scissors

eye chart

torch

medicine

aspirin

pills

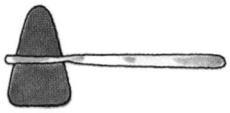

rubber hammer to make legs kick

tongue depressor for looking down throats

toothpaste

toothbrush

dental tools

tooth

tooth with a cavity

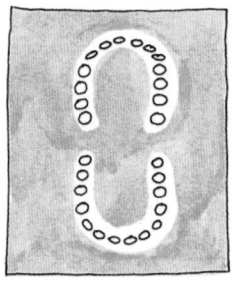

record chart to show where any cavities have been found

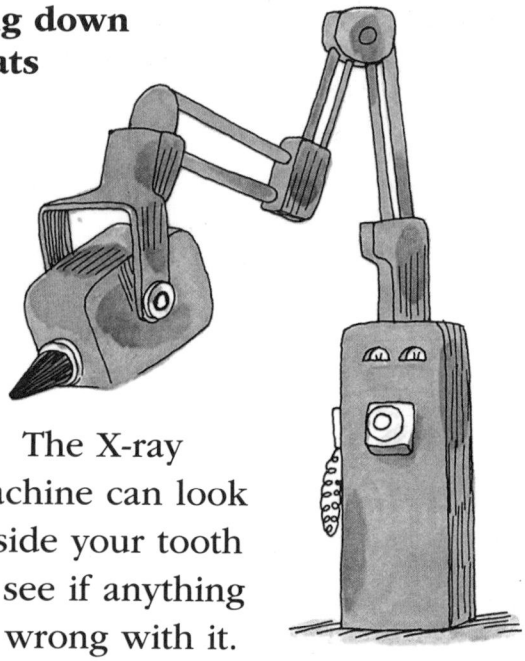

The X-ray machine can look inside your tooth to see if anything is wrong with it.

The doctor listens to your heart.

The dentist looks for cavities and the dental hygienist explains how to care for your teeth.

The Bear Twins Get Dressed

Kenny Bear wakes up one cold, frosty morning.
He wants to dress very warmly before going outside.
He yawns and gets up out of bed. He takes off his
pyjamas, folds them, and puts them in a drawer.

What should he wear today to keep warm?

pyjama top

pyjama bottoms

slippers

He puts on his

T-shirt

underpants

cap

shirt

trousers

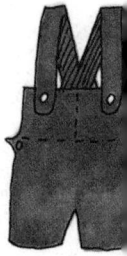

dungarees

tie

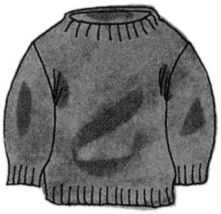

jumper

socks

hat

scarf

trainers

gloves

jacket

overcoat

raincoat

and rainhat.

As Kenny is walking out of the
front door his father says,
"Don't forget to put your boots on!"

boots

Kathy Bear stretches hard before she gets out of bed. She takes off her nightdress and hangs it on the hook in her wardrobe.

What do you think Kathy should wear today to keep warm?

nightdress

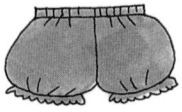

pants

vest

hair ribbon

She puts on her

blouse

skirt

jumper

socks

ear muffs

shoes

snowsuit

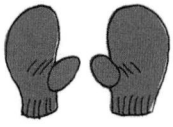

and mittens

She puts her purse

into her backpack.

As Kathy is walking out of the front door her mother says, "Don't forget to put your boots on!"

Do you ever forget to put on your boots?

deer
lion
elephant
tiger
panda
monkeys
polar bear
brown bear

At the Zoo

Mr. and Mrs. Mouse took their children to the zoo. How will the children ever be able to get all those balloons into their house tonight? Which is your favourite animal at the zoo?

The vet makes ure all the animals are healthy.

In the City

Mouse has just bought a book from the bookshop. She is going to buy a newspaper and then join her rabbit friends at the café and drink some lemonade with them. Show with your finger the way she will go. Remember to have her look both ways before she crosses a road.

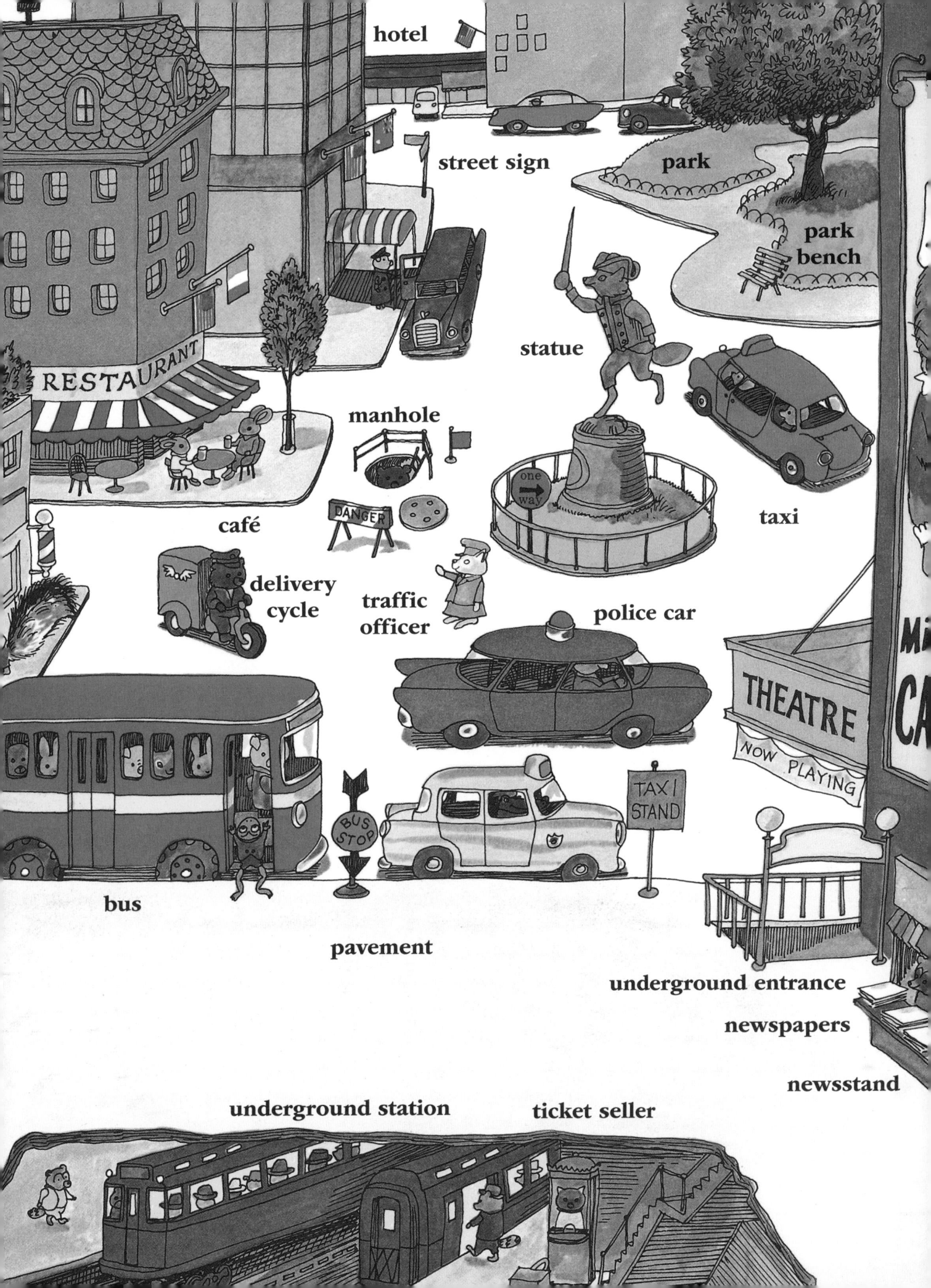
hotel
street sign
park
park bench
statue
RESTAURANT
manhole
one way
taxi
café
DANGER
delivery cycle
traffic officer
police car
THEATRE
NOW PLAYING
TAXI STAND
BUS STOP
bus
pavement
underground entrance
newspapers
newsstand
underground station
ticket seller

A Drive in the Country

There are many things to see when you take a drive in the country. Can you see Harry and Sally, the mountain climbers? Can you see what Harry has dropped from his backpack?

lighthouse
beach
fire lookout tower
crane
bay
drawbridge
woods
seaport
hill
tug
mountain
village
river
windmill
pond
log cabin
mountain climbers
cliff
road
forest
backpack
apple

Holidays

Holidays are happy times, aren't they?
Which holiday do you like best?
I bet you like them all.
On holidays we visit friends and relatives.
Sometimes we give or get presents.
What would you like to get for your birthday?

New Year's Day

St. Valentine's Day

Easter

Birthday

Halloween
moon
ghost
witch
skeleton
black cat
witch's broom
pumpkin
Hanukkah
trick-or-treat bag
angel
menorah
candle
wreath
Christmas
Christmas tree
stockings
holly
decorations
tree lights
beard
fireplace
sack
Father Christmas
present

At School

School is fun. There are so many things we learn to do. Kathy Bear is learning how to find a lost mitten.

pencil sharpener

pencil

fountain pen

ballpo pen

paper

chalk

notebook

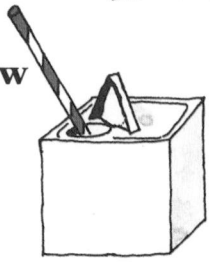

straw

milk

ink

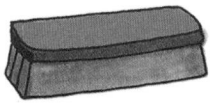

blackboard eraser

eraser

cookies

scissors

string

yarn

paper clip

glue

workbook

storybook

drawing pins

modelling clay

lost-clothing drawer

flag
clock
bell
blackboard
calendar
teacher
JANUARY
a b c
cat
dog
inkwell
map
map stand
wastepaper basket
artist
pupil
My name is Bob
desk
classroom
music teacher
paper shapes

refrigerator
kitchen cabinet
doorknob
can
opene
soap
teapot
socket
counter
freezer
bin
washing machine
dishwash
Father Pig
egg whisk
laundry
basket
eggshell
stool
Annie Pig
mixing bowl
spoon
measuring ju
rolling pin
Susan Pig
cookie cutter
dough
Peter Pig
sieve
cake pan
funnel
cookie tray
spatula
ketchup
bottle
flour bin
sugar bowl
mustard jar
food grinder

In the Kitchen

All the Pigs like to work in the kitchen.
They are making good things to eat.
What is Father Pig making?
What is Mother Pig putting into the oven?

When You Grow Up

What would you like to be when you are bigger?
Would you like to be a chef?
Would you like to be a doctor or a nurse?
What would you like to be?

sailor

nurse

taxi driver

police officer

firefighter

farmer

gardener

doctor

carpenter

musician

scientist

secretary

baker

dentist

chef

nger
artist
pilot
angler
truck driver
teacher
garage mechanic
reporter
photographer
shopkeeper
judge
librarian
dancer
daddy
mummy

Things We Do

There are many things that we can do.
And there are some things we cannot do.
What is the one thing we can't do?
Look and see.

dig

blow

build

break

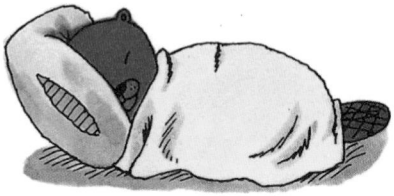

sleep

wake up

walk

run

stand

sit

read

watch

draw and write

pull
push
kick
talk
listen
shout
whisper
eat
laugh
smile
cry
drink
jump over
crawl under
fall down
we can't fly
peek
tip a hat
go up
go down
go in
come out

Work Machines

Busy, busy, busy bears. Most of the bears are busy moving dirt with their machines. But there is one bear who has a machine which does something else to the dirt. Which bear is it? What is she doing?

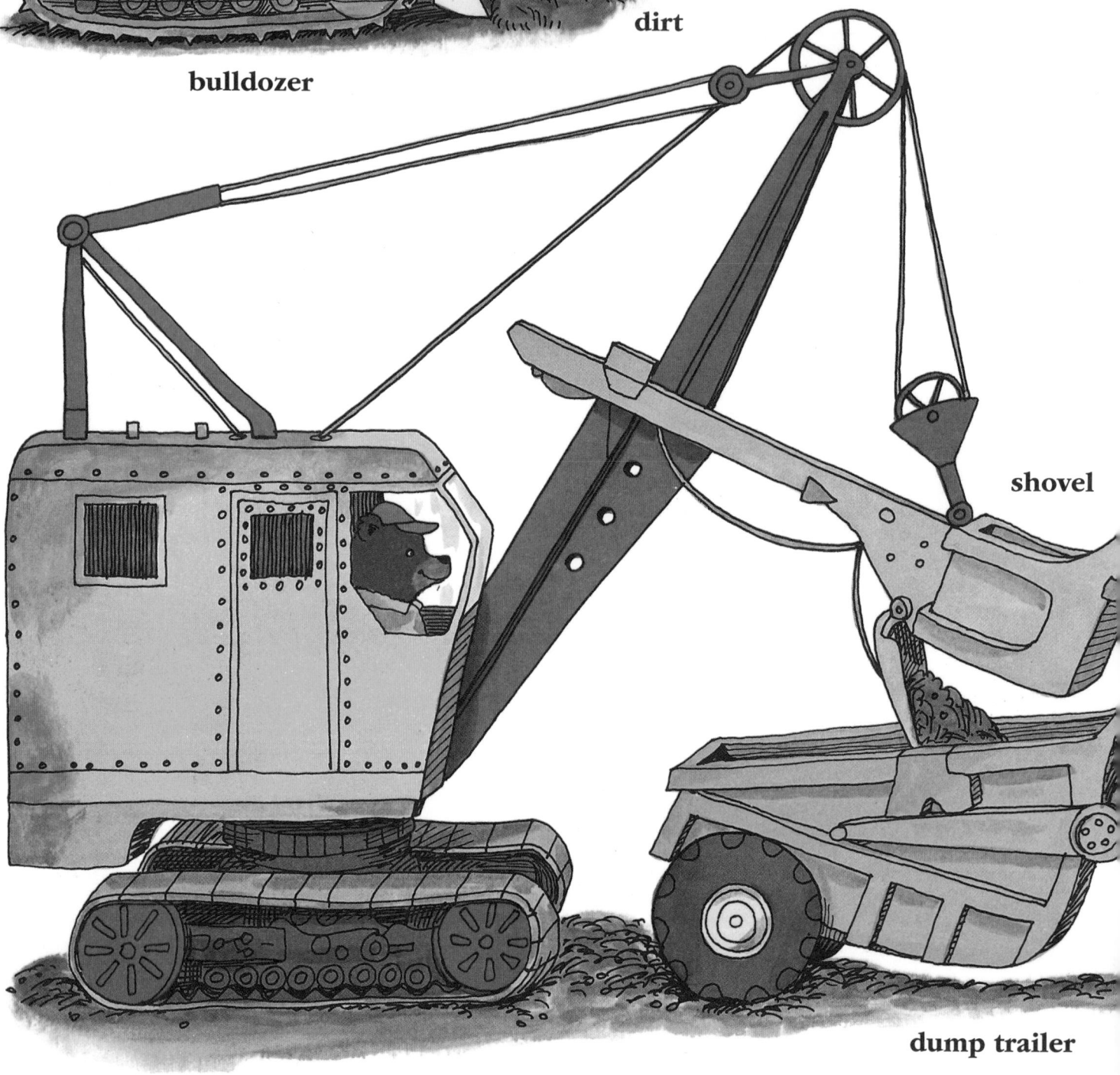

tractor scraper
tractor shovel
dump truck
bucket loader
dirt
roller
smooth dirt
and tractor
rough dirt

car transporter
PETROL
petrol truck
A
milk van
broken-down car
motorcycle
tow truck
TAXI
TAXI
taxi
sports ca

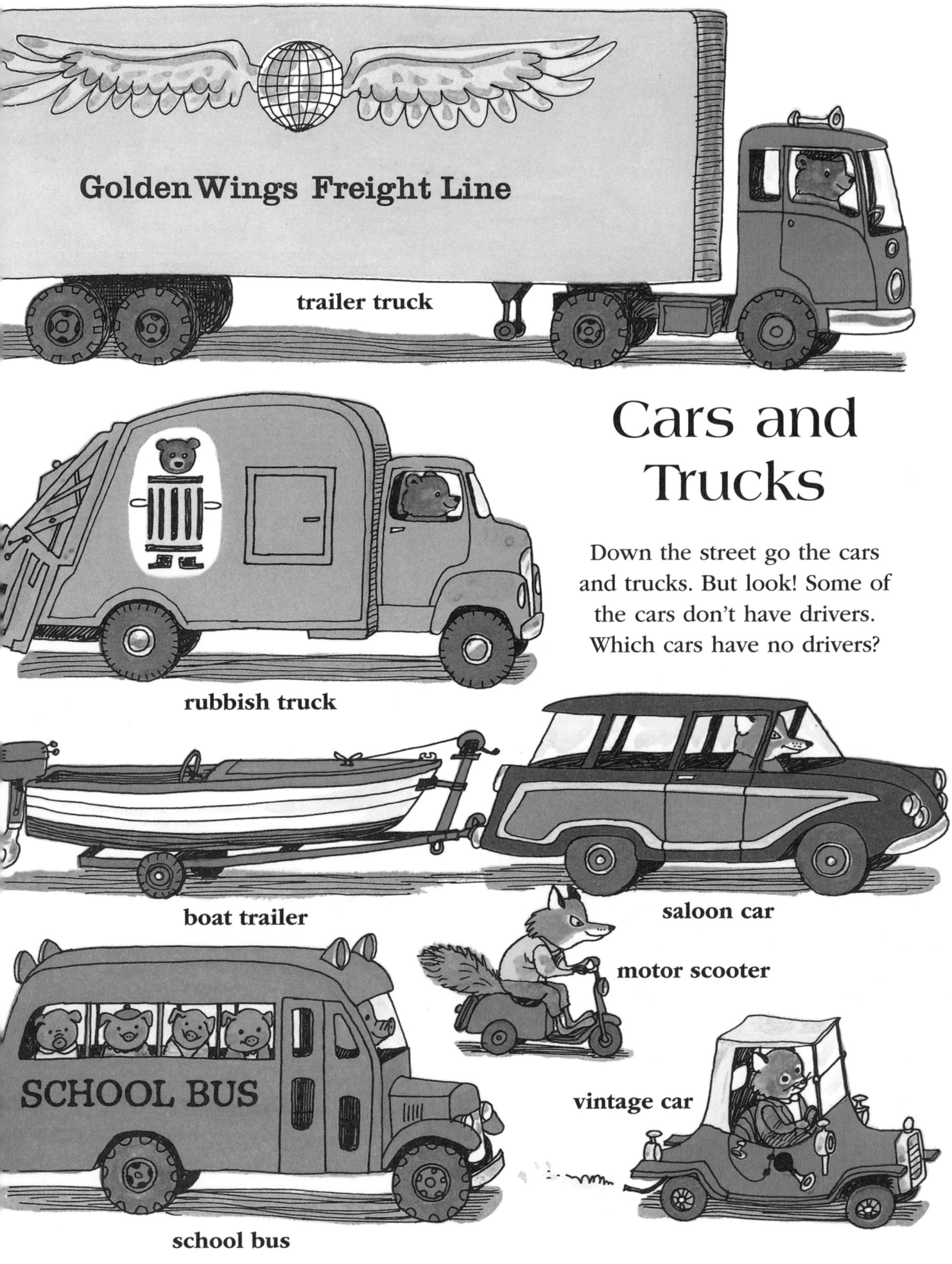

trailer truck

Cars and Trucks

Down the street go the cars and trucks. But look! Some of the cars don't have drivers. Which cars have no drivers?

rubbish truck

boat trailer

saloon car

motor scooter

vintage car

school bus

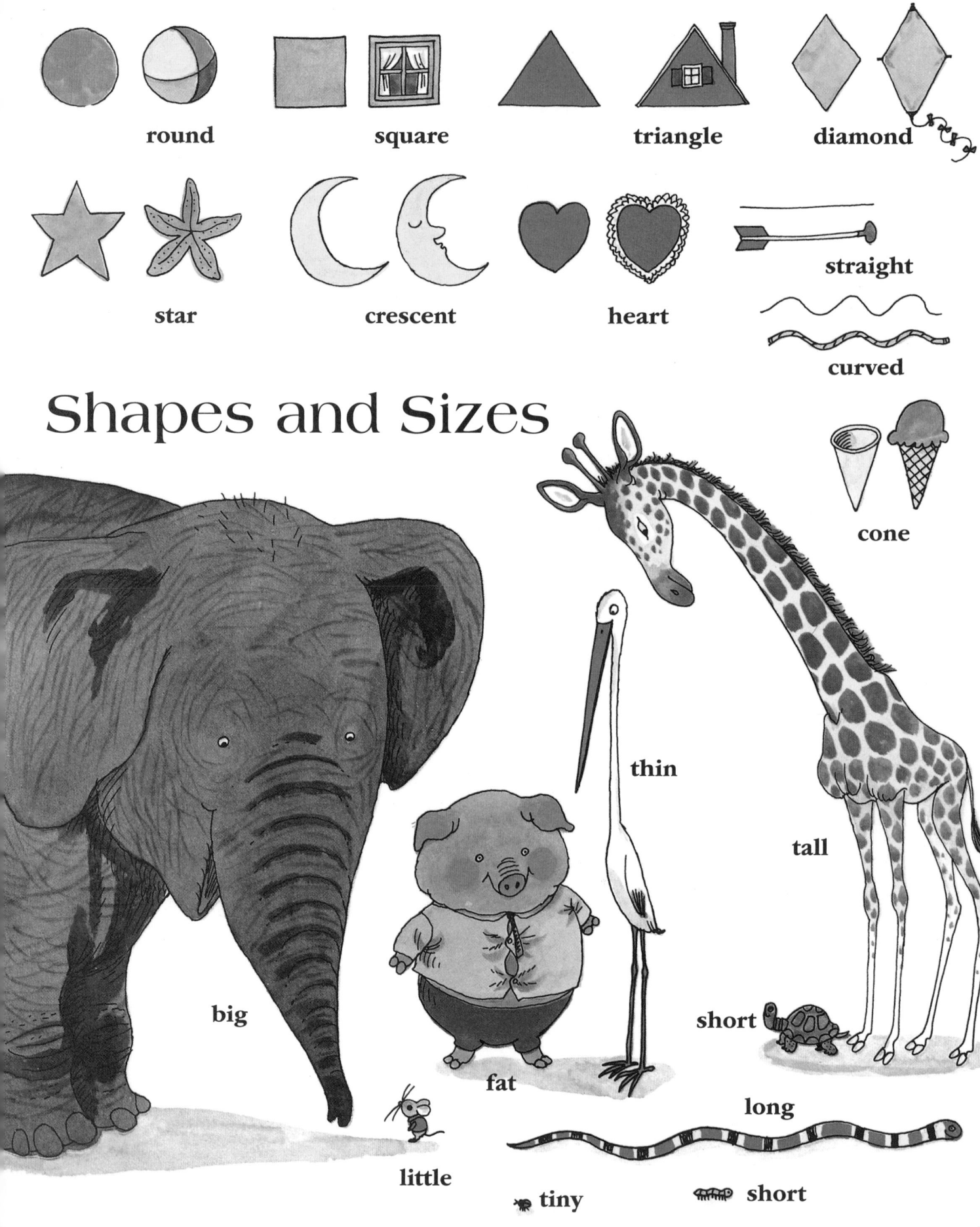
round
square
triangle
diamond
star
crescent
heart
straight
curved
Shapes and Sizes
cone
thin
tall
big
fat
short
long
little
tiny
short

father
mother
grandmother
The Baby
The Cat family has a new baby kitten.
They don't know what to name it.
What would you like to
name the new baby?
Write the kitten's name here.
uncle
ndfather
sister
rattle
baby
nappy
playpen
brother
bottle
aunt
cousin
pushchair
high chair
cot
Moses
basket
play table
walker
buggy

At the Circus

The band is playing and the animals are doing their acts.
What do you like to watch best at the circus?

flag
circus tent
trapeze
trapeze artist
safety net
acrobat
ticket seller
hoop
lion
cage
lion tamer
juggler
popcorn seller
EDDIE
sea lion
balloon seller

The Firefighters to the Rescue

Will the brave firefighters put out the fire in time? I think so, don't you?

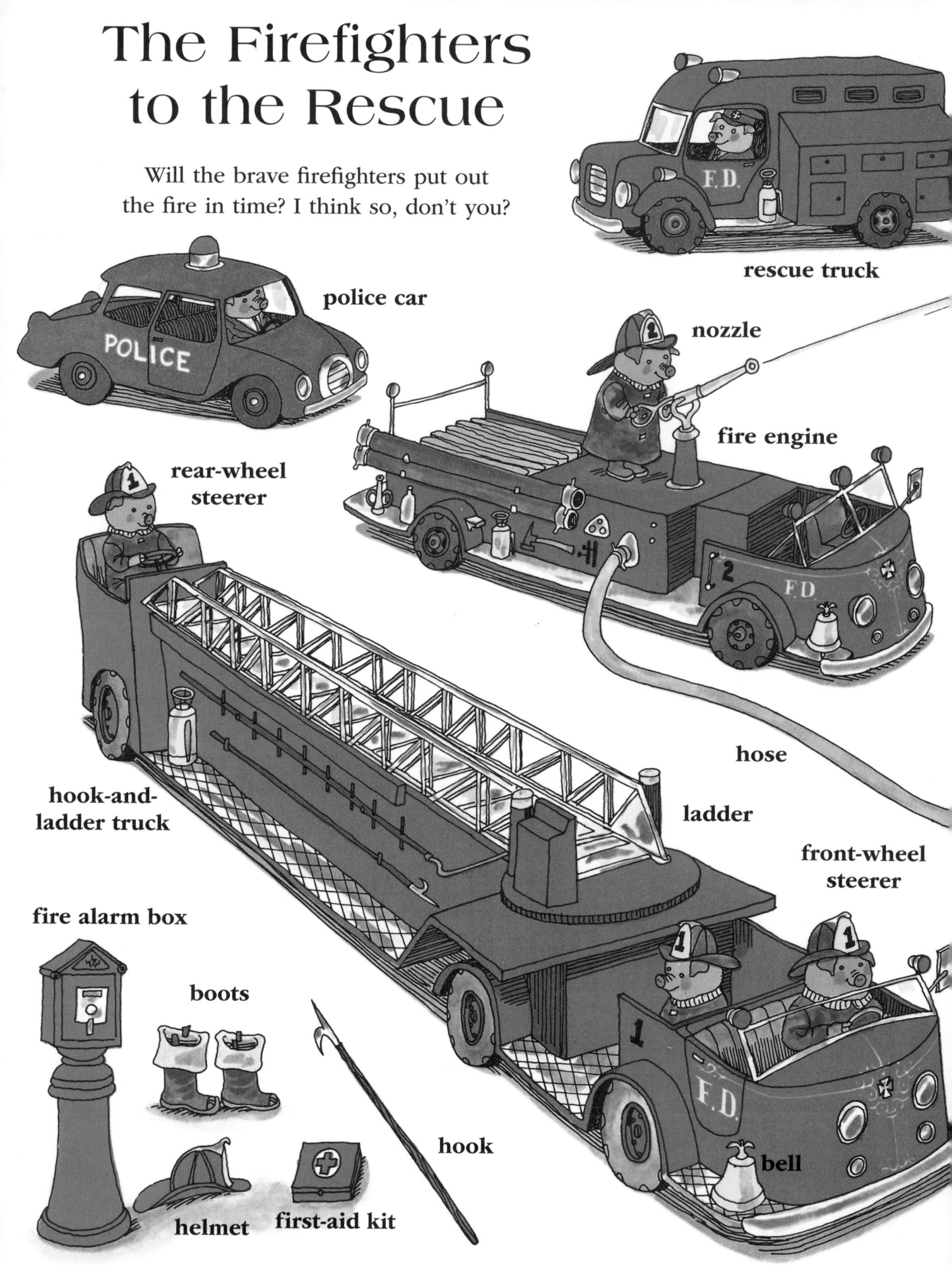

ambulance
F.D.
water
flames
smoke
fire chief
megaphone
cat in danger
CHIEF
F.D.
fire chief's car
pumper
firefighter
F.D.
3
fire hydrant
ladder
rescue net
firefighters
firefighter
fire
extinguisher

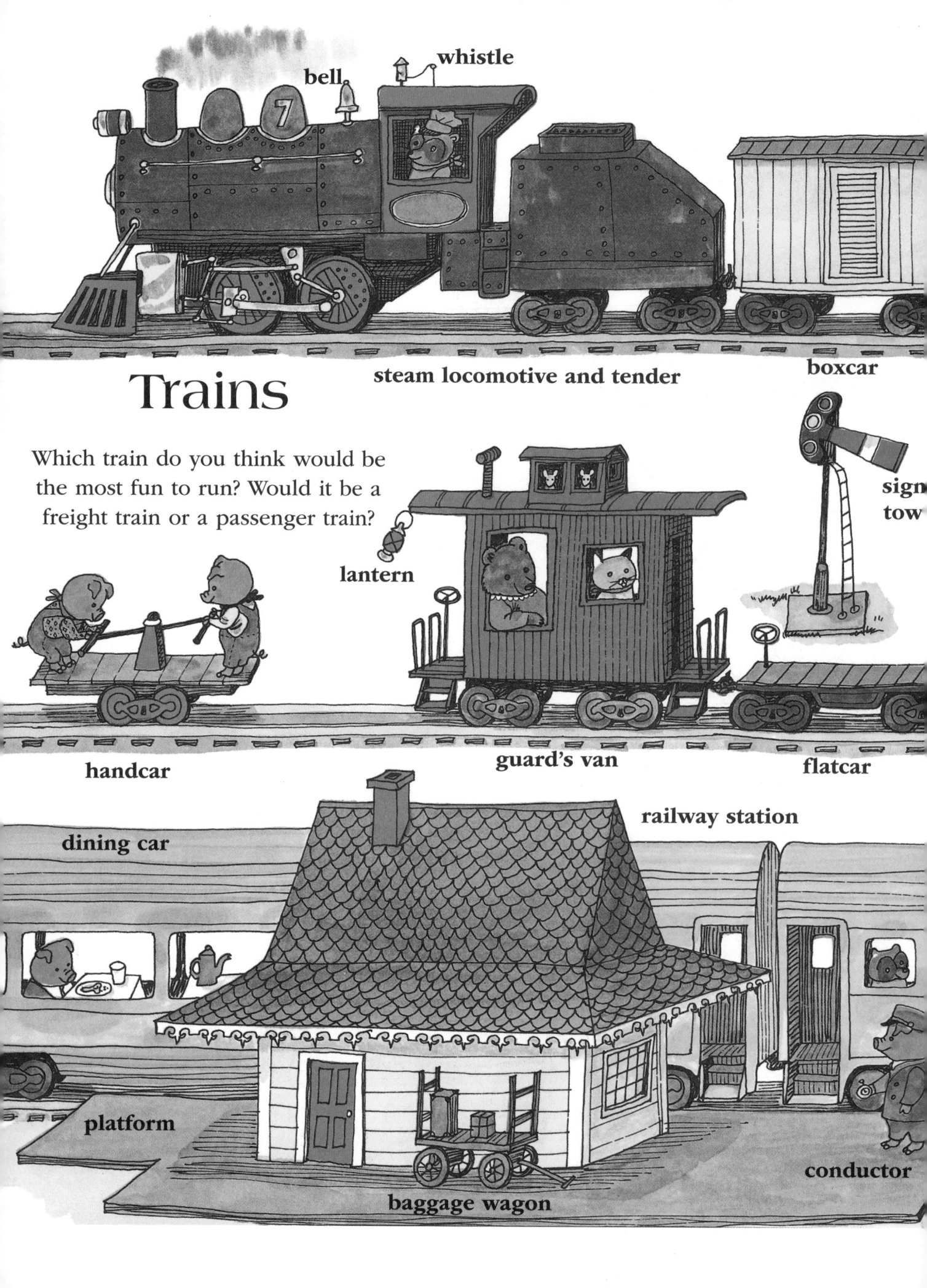
whistle
bell
7
steam locomotive and tender
boxcar
Trains
Which train do you think would be the most fun to run? Would it be a freight train or a passenger train?
lantern
sign
tow
handcar
guard's van
flatcar
railway station
dining car
platform
conductor
baggage wagon

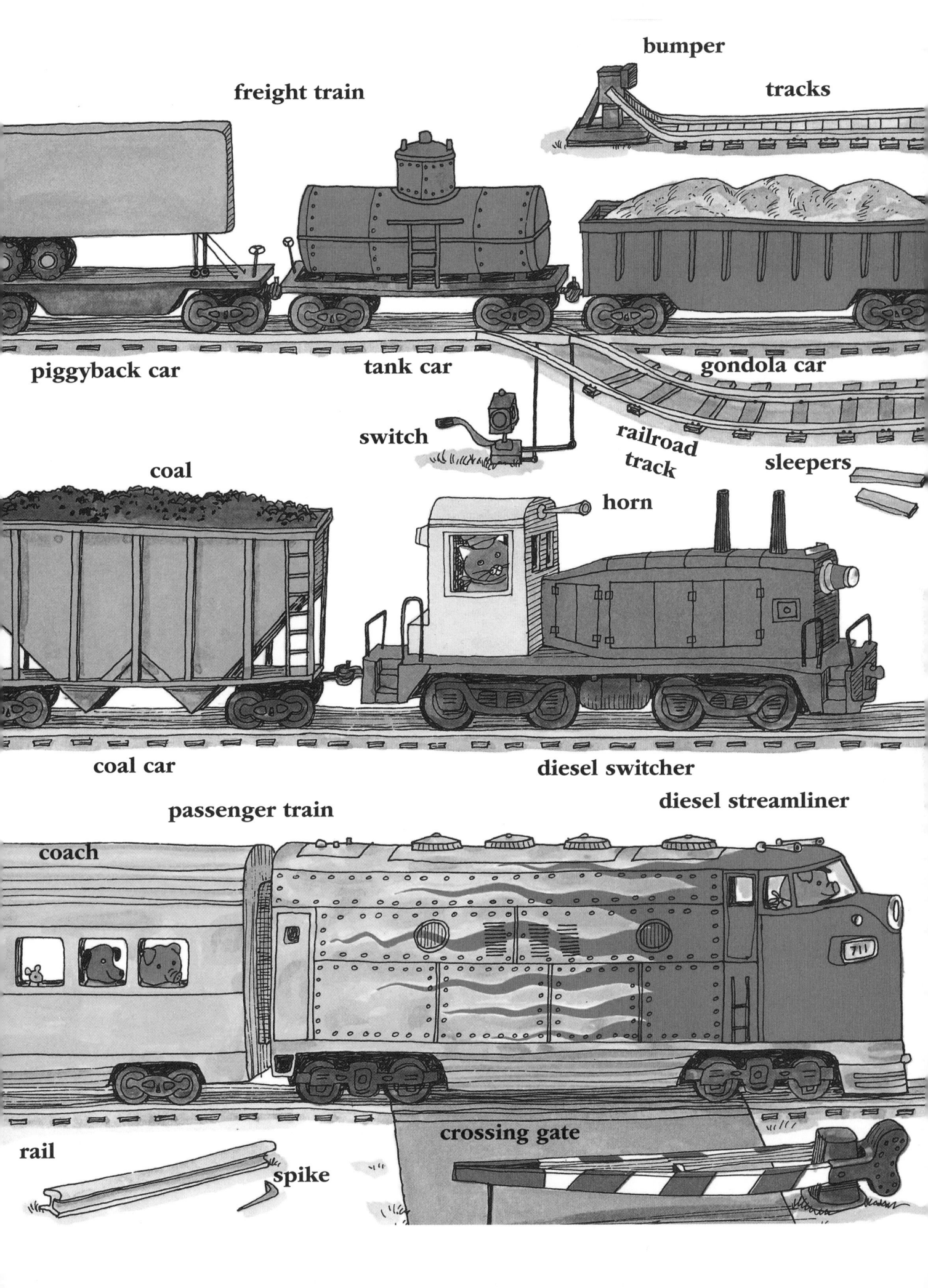
bumper
freight train
tracks
piggyback car
tank car
gondola car
switch
railroad track
sleepers
coal
horn
coal car
diesel switcher
passenger train
diesel streamliner
coach
711
crossing gate
rail
spike

At the Beach

In the summertime it is fun to go to the beach. What do you think Rabbit hears in the seashell? Is it the sound of the waves?

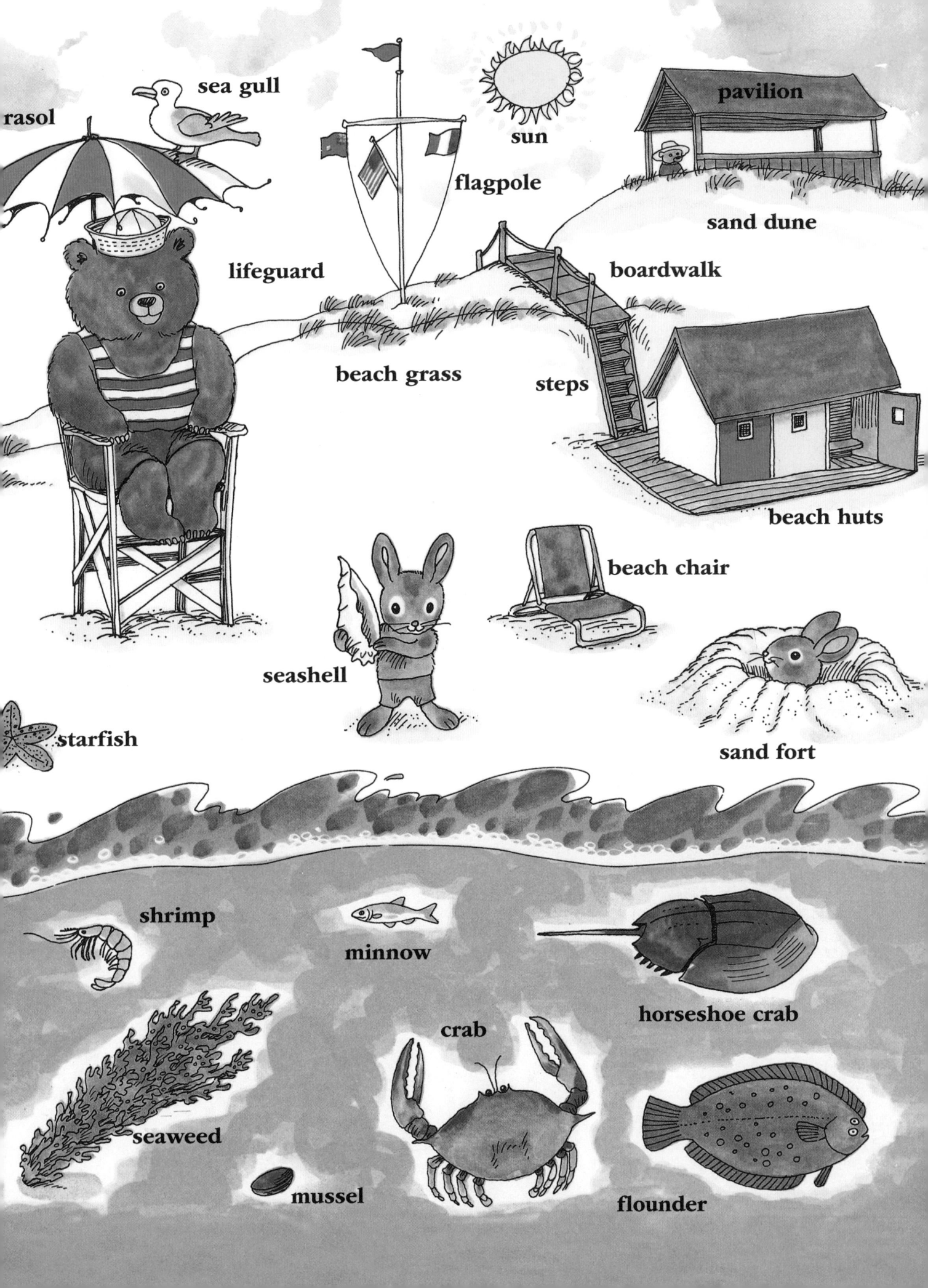
sea gull
rasol
sun
pavilion
flagpole
sand dune
lifeguard
boardwalk
beach grass
steps
beach huts
beach chair
seashell
starfish
sand fort
shrimp
minnow
horseshoe crab
crab
seaweed
mussel
flounder

Making Things Grow

Everyone is working in the garden.
Mr. Crow has a seed in his mouth.
Do you think he will plant it?
Or will he eat it?

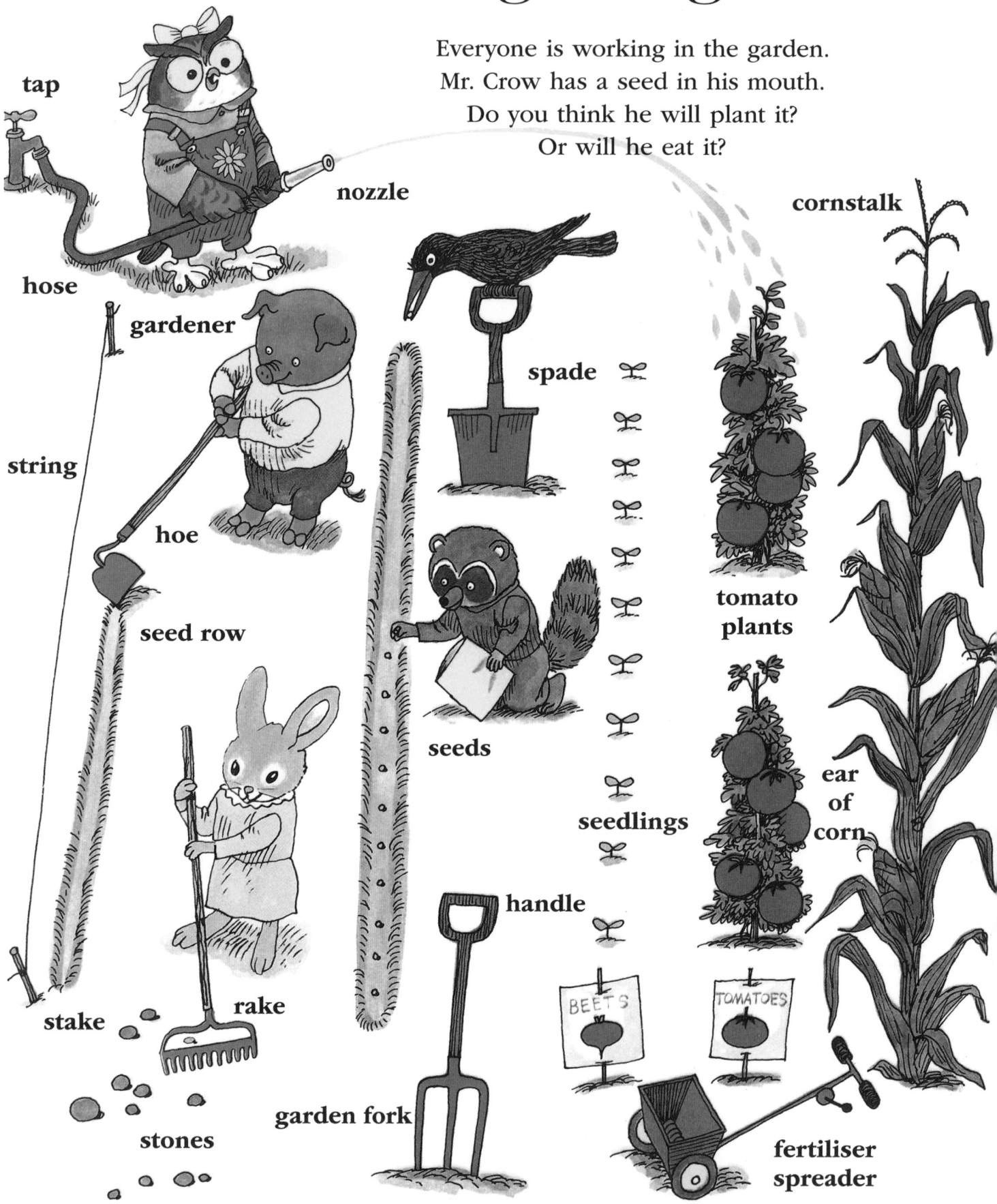

The Weather

When we go outdoors we see what the weather is like. Sometimes it is sunny. Sometimes it is cloudy. It can be windy, or cold, or hot. It can be snowing or raining. What was the weather like outdoors today? What is your favourite kind of weather?

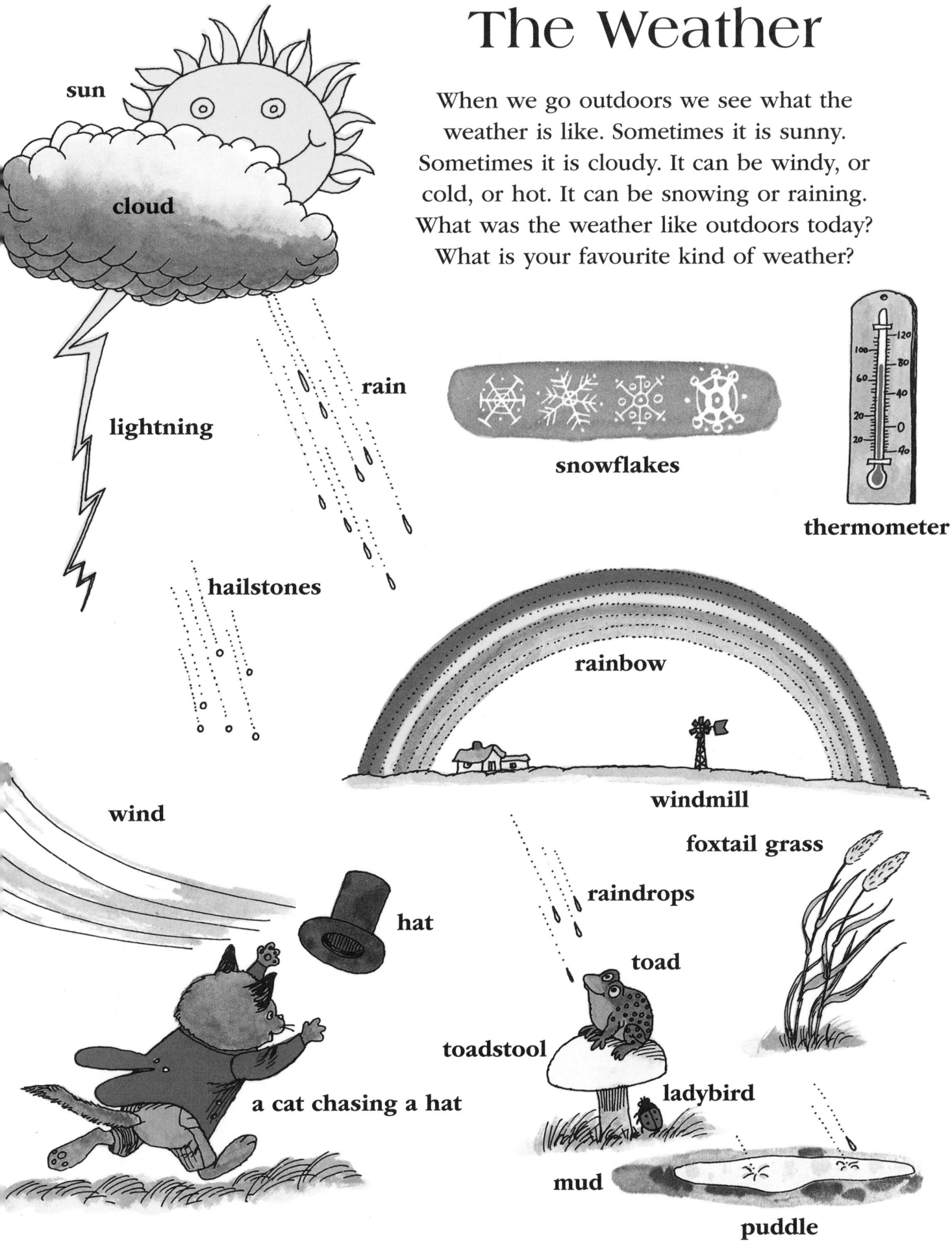

Spring

Look at that baby lamb hop!
It is spring. She is happy.
Look at Mr. Bear coming out of his cave!
It is spring. He is happy.
Now he can use his new lawn mower.

cow
meadow
calf
cornfield
fence
Summer
Do you like to go on picnics
in the summertime?
Ants just love to go to picnics.
Do you know why?
car
tent
fly
screen
barbeque
charcoal
picnic basket
cooler
hamburger
ketchup
charcoal bag
hotdog
mosquito
pole
paper cup
pickle
mustard
rock
ants
float
cattails
frog
deck
pond
water lily
dragonfly
pebbles
stones

Autumn

In the autumn the air gets colder. The green leaves turn to bright colours. Then they fall to the ground.

Winter

There are many ways to have fun on the snow and ice. Maybe you would like to do all of them. Would you?

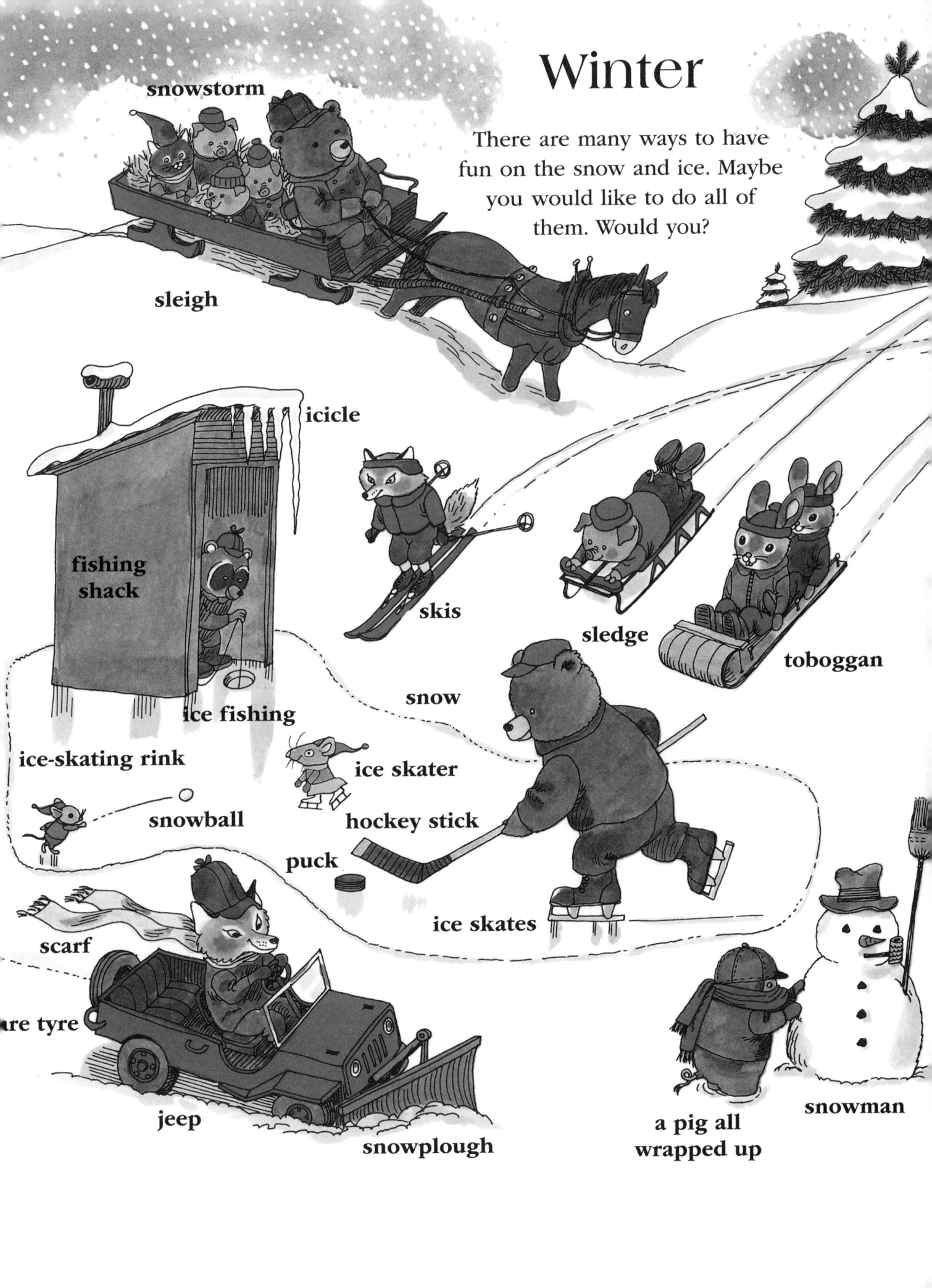

Little Things

Here are many little things.
What little things do you sometimes
put on your bedroom wall?

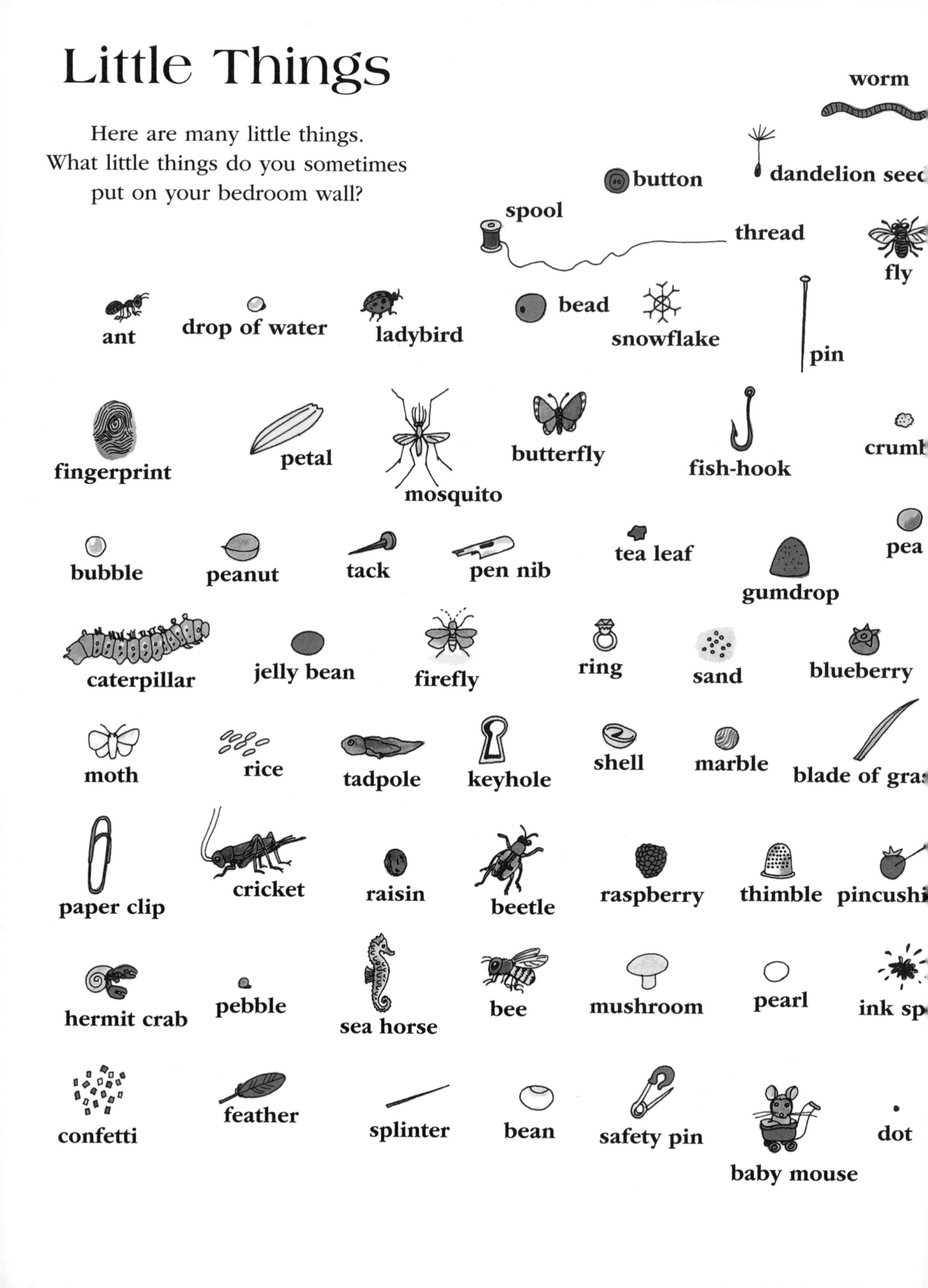

Parts of the Body

Bears use their paws to pick things up.
What do you use?

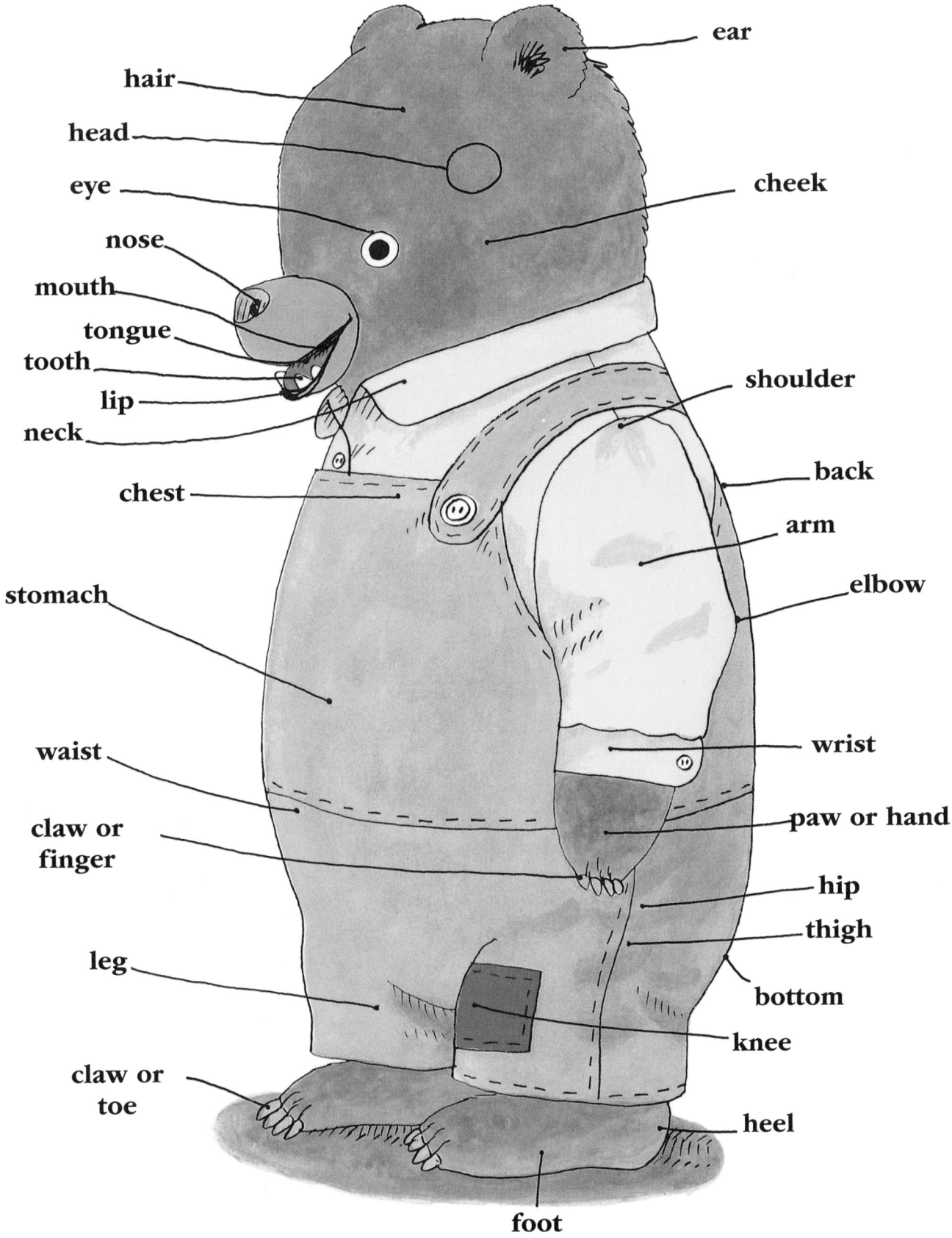

Bedtime

Little Elephant is getting ready for bed.
But who is that hiding under the bed?
Find that rascal and tell her to brush
her teeth and get ready for bed, too.

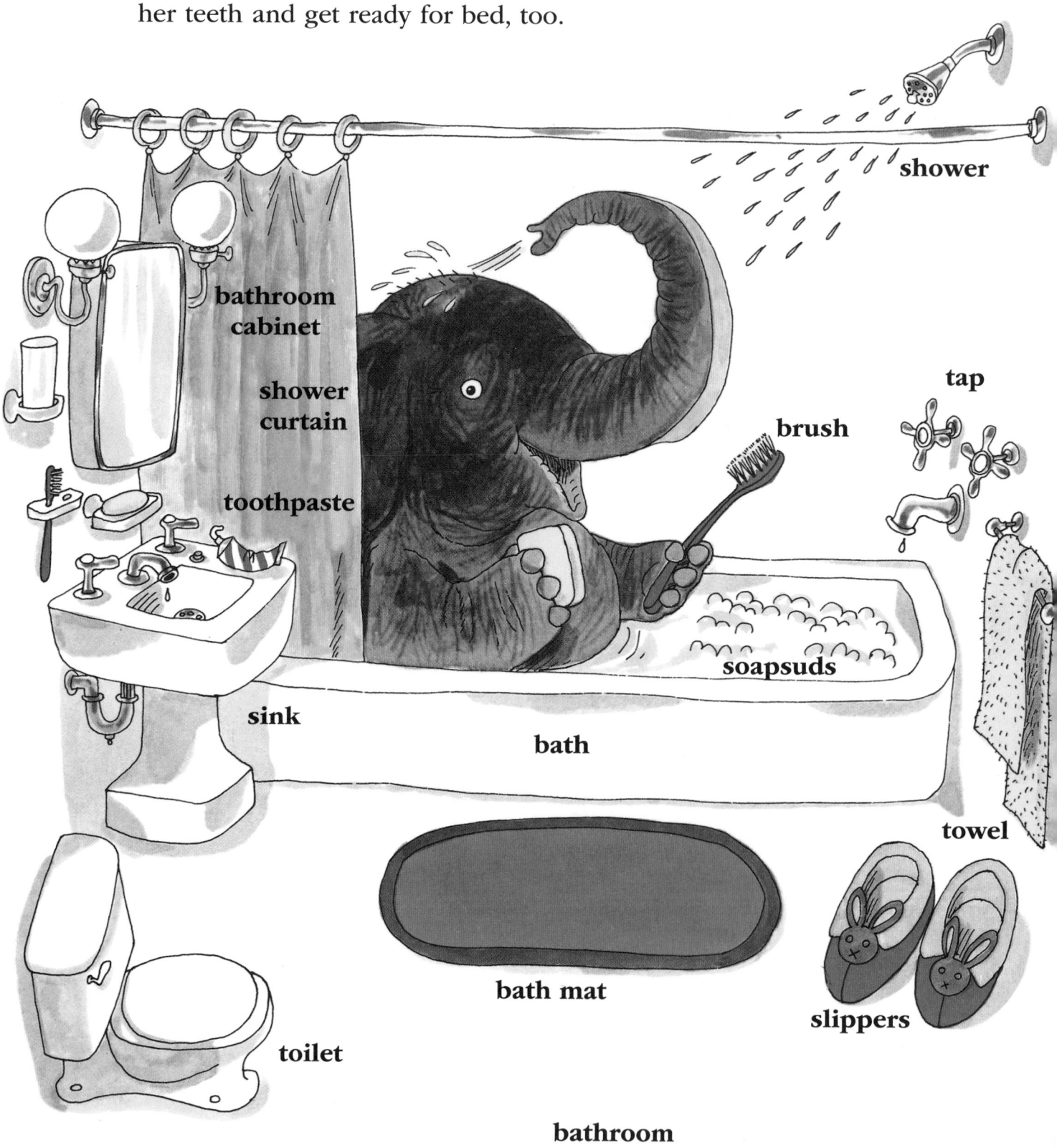

bathroom

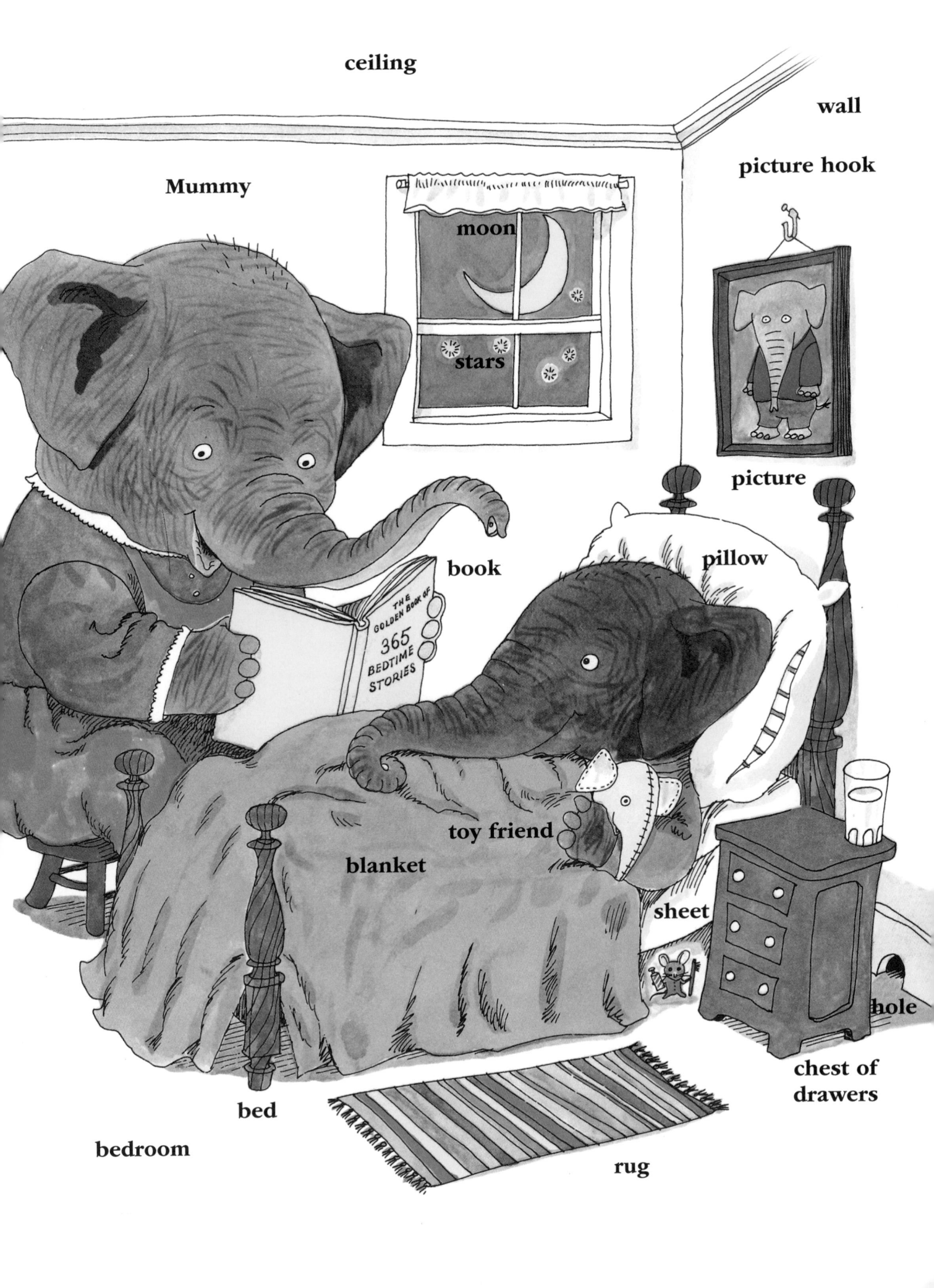
ceiling
wall
picture hook
Mummy
moon
stars
picture
book
THE GOLDEN BOOK OF 365 BEDTIME STORIES
pillow
toy friend
blanket
sheet
hole
chest of drawers
bed
bedroom
rug

Numbers

How high can you count?
Can you count up to twenty ladybirds?
I'll bet you can.

1 one whale

2 two walruses

3 three piggy banks

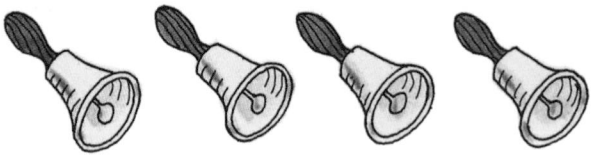

4 four bells

5 five grasshoppers

6 six eggs

7 seven caterpillars

8 eight spools

9 nine spiders

10 ten keys

11 eleven ants

12 twelve rings

13 thirteen gumdrops

14 fourteen leaves

15 fifteen snowflakes

16 sixteen acorns

17 seventeen pins

18 eighteen buttons

19 nineteen beads

20 twenty ladybirds